y differently / **v**

n / **vii**

k solid / **1**

War of words / **7**

Don't believe the hype / **15**

Tick, tick, boom / **21**

How to be a hero / **27**

The clone zone / **35**

The party spirit / **43**

Alienation / **51**

RS2: 8 Sessions

Based on the popular discipleship resource produced by

YOUTH FOR CHRIST

Authentic
LIFESTYLE

First Published in 2003 by Authentic Lifestyle

09 08 07 06 05 04 03 7 6 5 4 3 2 1
Authentic Lifestyle is an imprint of Authentic Media
PO Box 300, Carlisle, Cumbria, CA3 0QS, UK
and PO Box 1047, Waynesboro, GA 30830-2047, USA
www.paternoster-publishing.com

British Library Cataloguing in Publication Data
A catalogue record for this book is available from the British Library

ISBN 1-85078-482-5

Cover by 4-9-0 Ltd
Printed in Great Britain by
Bell and Bain Ltd., Glasgow

How to do Sunday differently

You are probably aware that, a few years ago, the general trend of cinema-going was in decline. The public were no longer willing to go to the local fleapit down the road to watch the only film on offer. To arrest this decline, cinema management started to do some serious thinking and realised that the problem was not the films themselves, but the environment and the choices that were being offered. As a result, cinemas started to do things differently, providing more choice of films, nicer seats, open areas for popcorn, drinks and games. And now, as I am sure you are aware, the number of cinema-goers is increasing dramatically.

In the Bible we have the best message to communicate - better than any blockbuster movie - but we need to realise that our audience has changed and the method by which we communicate also has to change and improve in order to arrest the decline of young people from the Church. RS2, YFC's discipleship programme for 11-14 year olds, is one such new method of communication.

The 11 year old is at an important point of decision-making and transition and we, as a Christian community, should be able to walk with them through this critical time. One of the biggest transitions is going from a small junior school to a massive secondary school. This is accompanied by going through puberty, doubts, faith, questions and some transitioning into adult roles, all taking place between the ages of 11 and 14.

RS2 is built on YFC's philosophy that one of the most important relationships for a person in this age group is that of the youth worker. This brilliant discipleship resource frees the youth worker to develop that relationship with credibility, innovative ideas, games, fun and teaching that targets real life issues.

If you are prepared to make the investment the return could be enormous. Who can tell what legacy you will leave? It is true that one significant adult can change a young person's perspective on all of life and particularly on their future years, but a personal relationship with Jesus can change them from now to eternity.

This book gives you a sample of the volumes that could be yours, as we produce ongoing material, written by several youth work practitioners, for each term of the academic year.

This could change the way you 'do Sunday' forever. In fact, you may end up not doing Sunday at all! I am aware that some churches have had to move the Christian teaching for their youth to other times in the week. This is due to social changes such as changes in family structure, weekend jobs for young people, parents working shifts etc.

What is clear is that where you do this and when you do this are not as critical as the fact that you do it - that you choose to make the material work - enabling evangelism and discipleship, which I believe are two sides of the same coin, to happen with this age group.

RS2 is a place in which 11-14 year olds can belong, where they connect with culturally relevant material that helps them make life choices based on Biblical teaching. RS2 provides the right atmosphere, the correct framework and brilliant material that will lead your group to grow in quality and quantity.

Roy Crowne, National Director of Youth for Christ in Britain.

Introduction

Welcome to this eight-programme resource, containing sample RS2 meeting plans. It is intended that they will serve as a taster to help local churches assess the potential for using RS2 with their 11-14 year olds on a more permanent basis.

RS2 has been borne out of the success of Youth for Christ's outreach programme, Rock Solid, which impacts in excess of 8,000 11-14 year olds each week.

RS2 has been produced for those who are a step on from Rock Solid, or who need something more than an outreach programme. It's geared towards 11-14 year olds who are already involved in a local church, interested in Christianity or wanting to know what it means to follow Christ in their early adolescent world.

RS2 works well on a Sunday morning, but it's not Sunday School - it's lots of fun, but it's not just entertainment - it provides weekly programmes, but it's more than a resource - it will not only keep them coming, it'll attract their friends as well.

Research clearly shows that large numbers of children and young people stop going to church between the ages of 11 and 14. This suggests that much of what is taught in Sunday School can lose its impact when the young people reach secondary school age. Young people in this age group need their own programme, in a style that accommodates them, with their needs in mind.

Although most churches who run RS2 do so as part of their Sunday morning set up, it can be made to work just as well midweek as part of a younger age youth group or cell group. You may even find it useful for your mid teens.

Whatever the setting, RS2 groups benefit from a continuous supply of meeting plans that are sent out each term. Each weekly programme is based around a particular theme and includes ice-breakers, interactive challenges, creative Bible studies, lively discussion, and with the occasional competition thrown in. Towards the end of each session there is a chance to reflect on what God might be saying to the young people as individuals, plus ways to get the whole group praying.

USING THE MATERIAL

As you will see by how the individual programmes are set out, there are three distinct segments to each session.

WWW.LOGON:

includes refreshments, introduction and announcements. This part of the meeting is very important as it enables the young people to mix in informally. Many adults are happy to go to a church service and leave as soon as it finishes, but most young people are only happy to be in a church setting if they get chance to interact with their friends.

WWW.BROWSE:

this is the main meat of the programme. It includes a theme game, Bible study, discussion, links and creative challenges. It's unlikely that you can include every element in a 45 minute - 1 hour programme (average Sunday morning time slot), so you'll need to 'cut & paste' a little.

WWW.SHUTDOWN:

how you conclude a session can be quite significant, therefore try and make sure that there is 5-10 minutes available for the group to reflect and pray.

Of course, different groups are at various stages in what they can accommodate and cope with. It is therefore up to leaders to tailor the material to what they're trying to achieve with their particular group.

THE 6 INGREDIENTS

We like to view RS2 as not just a resource, because it is as much about encouraging good practice for working amongst 11-14 year olds. The following are six principles that YFC believe are important for using RS2 to its full potential.

FUN & EXCITEMENT:

any youth work worth its salt has to include a high level of fun and enjoyment, particularly for early adolescents. We hope that your group find the RS2 sessions fresh and imaginative, but any programme for this age group should also include occasional trips out, camps and the chance to attend large scale youth events.

FRIENDSHIP:

you cannot imagine how important having friends is for the average 11-14 year old. Therefore Sunday mornings shouldn't be just about what you want them to learn, but creating an environment for them to relate.

LIFE SKILLS:

young people who were brought up to go to church want to know how relevant it is to follow Christ in the 21st Century. Does the Bible have something to say about the issues they're facing at their stage of life, today? As each RS2 meeting is based on a particular theme, they hopefully learn something of what it means to honour God in daily life.

GOOD NEWS:

Christianity is not bad news! It's not a set of rules to follow. It's not there as a back up for helping grown ups to get kids to behave. It's not primarily moral guidance. The whole deal is worked out as a person engages with a living God through a risen Saviour in the power of the Holy Spirit.

TEAM WORK:

RS2 (as with any resource) is only as good as the team using it. One of the main goals of YFC is to see thousands more Christians serving young people during this influential stage of life. How leaders relate to their group will have a major bearing on the impact of the programme.

PARTNERSHIP:

for an RS2 group to operate it has to be within the vision and ownership of local church. YFC will provide weekly programmes, training events, camps, support and access to additional resources, such as Youth Specialties products. There is also the benefit of networking with hundreds of other churches that are working with 11-14's in a similar way.

RS2 REGISTRATION

If you'd like to know more about how you can receive RS2 programmes on a termly basis and register to become part of the national network of groups, please contact Youth for Christ's Church Resource Department (0121 550 8055 or churchresource@yfc.co.uk).

rs 2

ROCK SOLID

MENU

We're precious to God

www.logon

Download	Refreshments
Network	Code Crackers
Mail	Intro and Messages

www.browse

Start-Up	The Price is Right
Mega Bite	1 Peter 2:4–8
Network	Social Reject
In-Put	Precious Stones
Chatroom	Long to Belong
Mega Bite	Before and After
Network*	Dream Come True
In-Put*	Dressed to Impress

www.shutdown

Save	Choice Challenge
On-Line	'Thank God!'
Close	

(SG) = small group activities, led by a member of the team.

****Eliminate for 45 minute programme.***

AIM TO TEACH

That we can trust Jesus with our whole lives, knowing he will never let us down. That truly believing in Jesus changes our lives.

AIM THAT THE GROUP SHOULD

Understand how God meets all our needs in Jesus. Consider their personal response to Jesus.

www.logon

00.00

DOWNLOAD... Refreshments

00.10

NETWORK... Code Crackers

PREPARATION: Put together 6 envelopes all containing cards bearing the following encoded words.

pcbh hfogv kvoh wg dfsqwcig

In pencil, on the inside of the envelope write **'A=M'**.

ACTIVITY: Divide the group into teams of four or five. Give each team an envelope, telling them that it contains everything they need in order to crack the code. (Most teams will probably discard the envelope).

They can solve the code by writing out the alphabet, and matching the letters as shown:

A B C D...

M N O P...

The decoded message reads **'DON'T TRASH WHAT IS PRECIOUS'**

00.15

MAIL... Intro and Messages

SAY: It's easy to throw away valuable things without even realising. When you get something new, you might throw away the instructions with the packaging etc. Some people do the same with Jesus – just brushing him aside without even realising how important he is.

Give this week's messages before opening in prayer.

Forward →

www.browse

00.20

START-UP... *The Price is Right*

PREPARATION: Bring a selection of interesting and unusual objects to display to the group. Make sure that at least one of them is more valuable than it might first appear.

ACTIVITY: Send two or three volunteers out of the room and display the objects to the rest of the group. Bring in the volunteers one at a time and ask them to decide which one they consider to be worth the most. When they have all had a go, tell them the true value of each item, dwelling on the most valuable.

Whilst in pairs, give 30 seconds to tell each other the following:

ö About the most valuable item they own

ö Something of what Jesus means to them/other people

SAY: The most valuable item could easily be mistaken for a piece of junk. How would you feel if you had thrown something out and later discovered how much it was worth? As we read the Bible we'll see that some people will have the same experience with Jesus.

00.25

MEGA BITE... *I Peter 2:4–8*

PREPARATION: Have a wastepaper bin strategically placed in the room, in which you have enough scrunched balls of paper for each group member to have their own. On one side of the paper they will find the Bible passage for the day.

ACTIVITY: Ask for two volunteers to look in the bin, and hand out its contents among the group. Then have a leader to read **1 Peter 2:4–8**, aloud while the rest of the group follow.

SAY: The key word in this passage is 'precious'. Jesus is precious to God and precious to those who believe. But others reject him. He must be one or the other.

00.28

NETWORK... *Social Reject*

PREPARATION: Divide the group into teams. Give each team some pens and a large sheet of paper.

ACTIVITY: Explain to the teams that they have four minutes to draw what they think of as the ultimate social reject – someone who doesn't fit in anywhere and would come bottom of most people's list of invites to their party (emphasise sensitivity). They should try to think of specific things that make people unacceptable (e.g. type of shoes) and label them on their picture. Then the person in each group with the most hair should come to the front to explain their 'social reject' to everyone else.

ASK: Do any of these things explain why Jesus is rejected?

SAY: People are often rejected for being regarded as boring, annoying, embarrassing, uncool and yet the truth is, Jesus Christ is none of these.

00.35

IN-PUT… Precious Stones

SAY: In this passage **(1 Peter 2:4–8)** Jesus is described as a capstone or cornerstone. These words refer to a large stone near a building's foundation which links several layers of smaller stones.

It can be hard work sometimes being a fan. If you tell everyone that some boyband mean everything to you, you might regret it. Five years later everyone thinks they are a joke. If we trust in something that lets us down, we can end up humiliated.

In a sense everything in the world is like that. Good looks become wrinkles, sports stars get injured, clever brains start to forget, even friends can let you down.

But look at how Peter refers to Jesus. He is the corner stone – a solid rock carefully laid, who we can trust in, who will never let us down so we'll never regret trusting him, **(verse 6)**.

00.40

CHATROOM… Long to Belong (SG)

PREPARATION: Put the group into threes and give each team a pen and piece of paper.

ACTIVITY: Allow 45 seconds to write down as many groups/organisations they can think of that they belong to. Using their imagination there can be quite a lot! Award a prize to the trio with the most genuine answers. You may discover some interesting things about your group members.

00.44

MEGA BITE… Before and After (SG)

PREPARATION: Take a large sheet of paper and divide it into two columns. At the top of the left hand column write 'before' and of the right hand column write 'after'.

ACTIVITY: Challenge the group to find all the changes Peter refers to in **1 Peter 2:9, 10**.

BEFORE	AFTER
No corporate identity	Belonging to God's people
Ordinary	Royalty
Far from God	Priests
Darkness	Light
Facing Judgment	Forgiven
Evil	Holy

Or alternatively, read the passage out loud and draw out its meaning by going straight into the next activity.

Forward →

00.48

NETWORK... Dream Come True (SG)

PREPARATION: Give each person in your group five small pieces of paper.

ACTIVITY: Ask them to try and picture what they imagine to be the dream of the majority of 11–14 year olds. They then write the five most prominent parts of that dream on the five sheets of paper.

They are not to confer, or give away their answers.

When everyone has finished, ask them to spread the papers out on the floor. Pile together those which convey similar ideas. Then, by finding which are the largest piles, identify the three most common parts of the 11–14's dream.

CONCLUSION: Amaze your group by showing how each of these aspects relates to:

Security – we want to feel safe. We want to know that our lives have a firm foundation and that when we wake up in the morning things will be alright.

Significance - we want to be valued. We need to know we are important to someone, that we belong and that we have a part to play.

ASK: How would you say God meets our needs for security and significance? **(REFER to 1 Peter 2:9, 10).**

00.53

IN-PUT... Dressed to Impress

PREPARATION: Do your best to find some lavish costumes and props for this final exercise.

ACTIVITY: Ask for a volunteer to act as a model!

SAY: If we put our trust in Jesus, the Bible says everything changes.

- We become royalty *(put a crown on their head)*
- We become priests *(put a robe round them)*
- We become holy *(use a halo made from wire)*
- We are chosen *(put a numbered football shirt over their head)*
- We belong to God *(put a chain over their neck with a pet-style medallion)*
- We are part of God's people *(give them a flag to hold)*
- We have been forgiven *(give them a scroll as a contract of freedom)*

Hopefully your volunteer will look a bit swamped and overcome, illustrating how many good things come to us in Jesus.

SAY: All this serves to show that God loves us and values us. We have a reason to live, a purpose to our lives – he makes available everything we need.

www.shutdown

00.58

SAVE... Choice Challenge

PREPARATION: Have appropriate music playing in the background and make pens and small pieces of paper available. Place the bin back in the middle of the room.

ACTIVITY: While the music is playing quietly invite the group to fetch a piece of paper and pen and write down three things they'd lose out on if they rejected Jesus Christ. Then to illustrate the loss further have them crumple their piece of paper into a ball and throw it in the bin.

SAY: Today we've looked at the choice to reject Jesus, and regret it later or to accept him as a precious saviour. We've seen how this choice will change everything in our lives.

We expect that not everyone in the group has yet made up their mind what to do with Jesus. That's okay! What matters is that you don't just chuck him away like you might with a piece of rubbish without stopping to take a good look at the difference he claims he would make in your life.

01.03

ON LINE... 'Thank God!' (SG)

PRAYER ACTIVITY: Have the group stand in one large circle. Take one of the crumpled pieces of paper from the bin and hold it in your hand. Explain that you're about to throw the ball of paper to someone in the circle who you want to pray a short prayer thanking Jesus for something he brings/wants to bring to our lives. Say that the prayer can be said aloud or silently in their mind, but when they've finished they should clearly say *'Amen!'* with everyone else responding *'Amen!'* The person who has just prayed throws the ball of paper to another person in the circle, and so on until everyone has had the chance to pray.

It'll be best if a leader prays first and sets the pace, so that the young people grab hold of the simplicity of the prayers you're referring to e.g. *'Thank you Lord Jesus that you offer us eternal life. Amen!'*

CLOSE...

End

2rs MENU

WAR OF WORDS

Learning to hold your tongue

www.logon

Download	Refreshments
Network A	knock Down
Network B	The Perfect Put Down
Mail	Intro and Messages

www.browse

Start-Up	Ganging Up
Chatroom	Victim Vote
Mega Bite	Murder???
Network*	Script Editors
Mega Bite*	Swap Shop
Chatroom	The Ultimate Upbuild
Chatroom	Prejudices

www.shutdown

Save	Cut it Out
On-Line	Throw Away Comments
Close	

SG) = small group activities, led by a member of the team.

**Eliminate for 45 minute programme.*

AIM TO TEACH

That using our words to insult is powerful and damaging. It grieves the Holy Spirit.

AIM THAT THE GROUP SHOULD

Consider what it feels like to be bullied. Seek forgiveness from those they have insulted. Ask God to help them improve their speech.

Forward

www.logon

00.00

DOWNLOAD... Refreshments

10.10

NETWORK A... Knock Down

ACTIVITY: Have everyone in the group find their own space in the room and hold one of their legs behind their back. On your command, the idea is that everyone hops around the room trying to stay balanced. People are allowed to knock into each other, but if anyone loses their balance they're eliminated. Play until the last person is standing. Have subsequent rounds if it goes all too quickly and the group are enjoying it.

NETWORK B... The Perfect Put Down (SG)

PREPARATION: Write out the following words on an acetate sheet, and then cut them out (one set for each team).

Stupid	Thick	Mental	Fat
Ugly	Skinny	Slag	Pervert
Nutter	Geek	Prat	Idiot
Cow	Pig	Slob	
Chicken	Soft	Dopey	Dizzy
Evil	Swot	Poser	Giddy

ACTIVITY: Divide the group into teams of four. Give each team a complete set of words and ask them to choose the five that would work together to create the most hurtful insult!

After two minutes, put an acetate sheet with an outline of an empty speech bubble on an OHP. Invite the groups up one at a time to construct their insult for the rest of the group.

DEBRIEF:

ASK: Why do some words get to us more than others?

ASK: Do you think that lads usually bully through insults more than girls do?

00.18

MAIL... *Intro and Messages*

SAY: Today we are going to take a look at insults, teasing and bullying.

Now you might think you've heard the message before; *'Don't be a bully, it's not nice.'* But as Christians we have far more to say about it than that.

Aggressive behavior has an impact far greater than most people realise. Life is vulnerable as it is, confidence is not always high and insults can knock us off balance. Some people have even attempted suicide.

www.browse

00.20

START UP... *Ganging Up*

PREPARATION: Try to get hold of some long pieces of rope or washing lines.

ACTIVITY: Put the group into teams of between 5–8 young people. Tie each group together, like tying a bundle of wheat with everyone facing outwards. Now give each individual the challenge of meeting and greeting at least ten other people, not including those that they're tied to.

SAY: It's good to stay within a group of friends, but this can also be a hindrance if we're not free to relate to other people or to be an individual.

A group of friends is a positive thing but not if we gang up on others.

The weakness of bullies is they're 'big' in a crowd but cowards when they're on their own – demonstrating that they're the weak ones.

00.25

CHATROOM... *Victim Vote*

PREPARATION: Make a recording (tape or video) of someone reading out the scripts below. These represent the testimony of victims of bullying, featured on a recent talk show. You could do it like TV with disguised interviewees (e.g. someone sitting behind a screen to hide their identity).

'I'm 6 foot 3. When I was 7 people thought I was 10 and expected me to act like a ten year old. I couldn't make friends. You were always visible when anything went wrong. I was sitting on the grass one day when someone came up to me and said, 'Oh, I didn't think you could sit down, because you'd never be able to get up again.' I still find it difficult to make friends, because you are always waiting for people to turn round and be nasty to you' (45 year old woman)

'I used to be overweight. I hated P.E. I'd always make some excuse not to get changed. When I did people would always shout 'Sumo! Sumo!'. I used to have epilepsy and get called 'Eppy'. I had to take drugs for epilepsy too, which used to make me drowsy, so people called me thick as well. Even now I'm very defensive. I don't let anyone get close to me. You want someone to get close to you, so you can tell them how you feel, but you can't. You're scared that people will take what you say and use it against you. You don't want to go through all that suffering again.' (25 year old man).

ACTIVITY: Ask everyone in the group to close their eyes. As they listen to the tape ask them to build a mental picture of the person speaking.

Then ask them to stand up to vote yes to the following questions:

- ö Do you think the person was male?
- ö Do you think the victim was a bit soft?
- ö Do you think the person was young?
- ö Do you think this is a normal reaction to bullying?

Forward →

DEBRIEF: We started the session by making insults and we tend to be quite good at it. It seems good fun most of the time and we probably don't really mean any harm.

Perhaps we think it would be a bit boring if we went round being nice to people all the time.

But as we've just seen, what we say can have devastating effects. But that's only half the story. Let's look at Jesus' views on the subject.

00.31

MEGA BITE... *Murder???*

READ: **Matt 5:21, 22**

SAY: In case you missed it; Jesus said, anyone who says ***'You Fool!'*** will be in danger of the fire of hell.

ASK: Do you think Jesus is being a bit strong here?

Now of course everything we believe about God's forgiveness still stands. But Jesus' words make people stop and think. Most people think they're not too bad because they haven't murdered anyone. But Jesus indicates that if you try to put down another human being with your words you are guilty of sin for which the consequences are just as serious.

00.34

NETWORK... *Script Editors*

PREPARATION: Record an episode of Eastenders or the The Simpsons and pick a suitable two minute clip that contains a lot of negative words or conversation.

ACTIVITY: Divide into teams of four. Explain to the group that you're going to play the two minute clip and you'll stop the tape when any group shouts out 'stop.' They should only shout 'stop' when something insulting is said or gestured. At this point teams should write down what they saw as being negative. Leave a few seconds before turning the tape back on again, letting it run until told to 'stop.' The idea is for teams to pick up all the negatives they can.

Quickly check that they have identified all the insults etc, and announce the winners.

Offer breath freshening chewing gum to the winning team.

DEBRIEF:

SAY: If you removed from the clip everything which was unhelpful or aggressive or insulting or untrue, or vulgar, what percentage of the clip would be left?

In the case of The Simpsons it's usually quite funny, but in real life it isn't.

Now Jesus says if we even call someone a fool, we are like murderers. We might reply, *'Come off it! That's a bit strong! I mean who never calls someone an idiot?...'*

But that's the point. We are all guilty. And it is serious. It is serious because every person is highly valuable to God.

00.42

OMEGA BITE... *Swap Shop*

SAY: In this bit of the Bible we find Paul in the middle of a long description of the changes that should occur in the life of a growing Christian. Here he is concentrating largely on the things we say and the attitudes that lie behind them.

READ: **Ephesians 4:29–5:2**

PREPARATION: Form a set of A4 cards each with a loop of string attached so as to be worn as an oversized medallion. On the cards write the following words in pairs, one on each side.

LIES	TRUTH
IMPURITY	PURITY
STUPID TALK	HELPFUL TALK
RUDE JOKES	THANKSGIVING
BITTERNESS	FORGIVENESS
RAGE	COMPASSION
ANGER	LOVE
BRAWLING	KINDNESS

ACTIVITY: Ask for two volunteers. Use them as props as you explain the changes that God wants us to make.

SAY: In this passage we discover two things that God wants us to get rid of and two things to replace them.

UNWHOLESOME TALK – Hang the cards on your first volunteer showing lies, impurity, stupid talk, rude jokes.

Instead everything that comes out of our mouths should build people up (turn the cards over one at a time).

VIOLENT BEHAVIOR – Hang cards on your second volunteer showing the words bitterness, rage, anger, brawling.

Instead we are to be kind and compassionate, like Jesus, who even offered forgiveness to those who were putting him to death (turn over the cards one at a time).

00.47

CHATROOM... *The Ultimate Upbuild*

PREPARATION: Give each team five small pieces of acetate sheet and an OHP pen.

ACTIVITY: In a reverse of 'THE PERFECT PUT DOWN' give pairs two minutes to come up with their best attempt at encouraging words. They should try hard not to make it cheesy or to sound insincere. They should choose carefully the words which they feel would be most encouraging to hear, write them down (on the acetate pieces), and be prepared to show the end result on the OHP screen.

00.52

CHATROOM... *Prejudices*

SAY: We all have things which we dislike in other people, that is in our human nature. Ask the members of your group to identify their pet prejudices. You can start them off with these suggestions! Swotty people, spotty people, immature, untrendy, trendy, arrogant, aggressive etc.

Go round the group and ask them to think of one thing they take a natural dislike to and why. Encourage them to be honest, but not proud of their prejudices! (but only do this if the group can cope with not being offensive to people there).

www.shutdown

00.55

SAVE... Cut it Out

PREPARATION: Give each person 2 blank sheets of A4 paper.

ACTIVITY: Encourage the group to close their eyes in an attitude of prayer and to think back to the TV clip from earlier in the meeting. Ask the group how much they think God might want them to cross out from their everyday speech?

To illustrate this, give them 60 seconds to silently pray and to allow the Lord to speak to them. Then as an act of commitment to God, rip from the sheet a section which shows how much they want to change (with God's help) of their regular speech.

Have the group repeat the exercise with their second sheet of paper, but on this occasion the torn off piece should illustrate the amount they want God to bring 'healing' from negative remarks made to them

00.58

ON LINE...Throw Away Comments

PREPARATION: Place a bin in the centre of the room.

ACTIVITY: Encourage everyone to crumple up their two torn off pieces of paper into paper balls and to throw them into the bin. With everyone standing around the bin, have them close their eyes whilst a leader closes in prayer by committing the two issues to the Lord.

CLOSE...

End

rs 2 MENU

DON'T BELIEVE THE HYPE

The truth about happiness

www.logon

Download	*Refreshments*
Network	*Memory Madness*
Mail	*Professor Brainwave and Messages*

www.browse

Start-Up*	*Happiness Is*
Chatroom	*The Essential Selection*
Mega Bite	*I Don't Believe It! (part 1)*
Network	*Happy Ever After*
Mega Bite	*I Don't Believe It! (part 2)*

www.shutdown

Save	*Moments of Glory*
On-Line	*Reasons To Be Cheerful*
Close	

(SG) small group activities, led by members of the leadership team.

**Eliminate for 45 minute programme.*

AIM TO TEACH

That 'Money makes you happy', 'If you live life right you'll be happy all the time', 'You don't need God when you're happy' are all lies.

AIM THAT THE GROUP SHOULD

Learn the value of contentment, consider how they might deal with changing emotions, take away some reasons to thank God everyday

rs 2

Forward

www.logon

00.00

DOWNLOAD... *Refreshments*

As you serve refreshments this week, carefully choose two types of music. Play one or two songs of an up tempo and fun nature. Then play one or two that are more angry and aggressive.

00.10

NETWORK... *Memory Madness*

PREPARATION: Place on a tray a selection of items that would represent something that might make some people happy. Make sure that you include items that are a variety of sizes, shapes and colours.

ACTIVITY: Give each person a pen and piece of paper. Have a leader bring the tray into the room with a cloth covering the items. Explain to the group that the cover is going to be removed from the tray for forty five seconds and they need to take a good look at the tray's contents. After the forty five seconds are up, have the tray covered and give people two minutes to write on their paper as many of the items that they can remember.

The winner is the one who can record on paper the most items.

00.16

MAIL... *Professor Brainwave and Messages*

Dress your 'team analyst' in a wig, glasses and a lab coat and have them enter the room, introducing them as a professor of psychology, specialising in human behaviour.

Explain that they have just been part of an experiment and they can now announce the results:

THE HAPPY MUSIC PRODUCED CERTAIN KINDS OF BEHAVIOUR:

Point to one or two people who look happy. Describe any leaders who are famous for bounding up to people and greeting them enthusiastically. Suggest possible reasons that may have led to their behaviour, being in love, having too much coke or caffeine, completing their collection of Barbie clothes, remembering to get dressed before leaving the house.

THE SAD MUSIC PRODUCED A CHANGE IN BEHAVIOUR:

Describe the general mood of the group. Suggest possible reasons that may have led to their behaviour: getting out the wrong side of bed, having to put on the same pair of socks for the fourth day running, their football team losing the day before. Refer to some people in the group by name who stood out as they mingled. Be careful not to offend.

Thank the professor and point out how strange it is that things can influence how we're feeling without us even knowing it.

www.browse

00.20

START UP... *Happiness Is*

Divide the group into 4's. Give them ten minutes in their groups to devise a TV commercial with the slogan 'Happiness is...' and then the name of the product. The products can be real or fictitious.

Ensure that every member of the group takes part in performing the advert.

You could start off by showing a series of videoed adverts to inspire them.

Have the groups act out their commercials in turn.

00.35

CHATROOM... *The Essential Selection*

PREPARATION: Write out the following phrases on separate pieces of card. If you have time cut the edges of the card to make them look like pieces of a jigsaw puzzle. Put them up on a wall or board.

Designer labels	A family car	Food
Holidays abroad	Shoes to be proud of	A bed
TV	Make up	A Mobile Phone
Comfortable sofa	Pot Noodles	Running Water
Your own bedroom	A washing machine	A shower
Electricity	A fridge	Neighbours
A dishwasher	A garden	School Uniform
Football	God	Music

ACTIVITY: Place a large bin in front of the group and label it non-essentials. Read the cards out one by one and ask the group if the items represent essentials for happiness. Take any non-essentials off the wall and toss them into the bin. After they have worked through all the items, read out all those remaining on the wall, as the group's verdict on what is essential for a happy life.

00.40

MEGA BITE... *I Don't Believe It! (part 1)*

Write the following statement on a large flash card. 'Money Makes You Happy'.

SAY:

- Much of the way people live is based on this assumption.
- Even now you are taking your first steps. At school there is a pressure to do well, to get good grades so that you can get onto the right college course so that you can be well qualified to get a well paid job which will keep you secure and make you happy.
- It's a lie. And it's important to realise it as soon as possible.

READ: **1 Timothy 6:6–10**

SAY: Money is great. But our love for it can mean trouble.

ASK: What are the dangers of loving money?

- ö Falling into a trap.
- ö Foolish and harmful desires.
- ö Ruin and destruction.
- ö Wandering from the faith.
- ö Piercing yourself with grief.

SAY:

- ö Happiness does not depend on money.
- ö If we think happiness will arrive when we reach a certain level of wealth we will be disappointed.
- ö What makes you think you'll be satisfied when you get more money?

00.45

NETWORK... *Happy Ever After*

Give each group member a piece of A4 paper and a pen. Put up an OHP or equivalent with the following headings:

- ö Once upon a time there was a (boy's name) .
- ö Who met (girl's name).
- ö At the (place or event).
- ö He said (boy's words).
- ö She said (girl's words).
- ö And they decided to (the consequence).

Play a game of consequences, where the group members write their choice of boys name, fold the paper to conceal what they have written and then pass it to their neighbour for the girl's name, and so on until the story is complete.

Have some of the group read out their stories.

00.50

MEGA BITE... *I Don't Believe It! (part 2)*

Hold up a second flash card with the statement *'If you live life right you'll always be happy.'*

SAY: Many of us think, that if only our circumstances would change, then we'd suddenly have a life of happiness, it's somewhere around the corner and we just need to find it.

READ: **Psalm 10:2–6**

SAY:

- ö In this psalm, the man who thinks he'll always be happy is described as wicked and arrogant.
- ö Thinking you've got life sussed often goes alongside greed, pride and boasting.
- ö It's this attitude to life that has no need of God. If we are conscious of God, we know that there will be times when we mess up, when we learn through suffering, and when our faith is tested. But this is important so that we can mature and get stronger.

www.shutdown

00.54

SAVE... Moments of Glory

Write out the following events on separate pieces of card. Give one to each member of your small group. Ask each group member in turn to mime celebrating the event on the card. Give the rest of the group 45 seconds to guess the event. Remember – they are not to mime the event, but the celebration afterwards!

Scoring a goal	Passing a driving test	Winning an election
Getting married	Landing on the moon	Discovering buried treasure
Finding a bargain	Finishing a jigsaw	Winning a war

With soft music playing in the background ask individuals to right down (or chat in pairs) three occasions they can remember celebrating in similar fashion to the above.

01.03

ON LINE... Reasons To Be Cheerful (SG)

SAY: We can't be happy all the time. But there are always good reasons for Christians to celebrate. Try these for size! (Have the following written up on a board):

- ö I have a Father who loves me.
- ö All my sins are forgiven.
- ö I am going to Heaven.
- ö God's spirit and power lives in me.
- ö God has a plan for my life.

Have a leader to close in prayer based on the above.

CLOSE...

TICK, TICK, BOOM

MENU

Agro

www.logon

Download	Refreshments	
Network	Release The Pressure	
Mail	Intro and Messages	

www.browse

Start-Up	Slo-mo Charades	
Mega Bite	Slow To Anger	
Network	Count To Ten	
Mega Bite	Quick, Slow, Slow	
Chatroom*	Wind Up Classics	

www.shutdown

Save*	Smoothing It Over	
On-Line	Letting It All Out	
Close		

(SG) = small group activities, led by a member of the team.

*Eliminate for 45 minute programme.

AIM TO TEACH

That anger is not wrong in itself, but needs to be controlled. That we, like God, should be slow to anger. That anger if harboured can give the devil a foothold.

AIM THAT THE GROUP SHOULD

Examine their own anger and it's causes. Uncover and confront any harboured anger in key relationships

Forward

www.logon

LEADERS NOTE...

The issues covered in this session can be covered meaningfully without upset. However, there may be members of your group who are very much in touch with things that have hurt them, and this session could trigger off some powerful emotions. Go gently, remembering that while most of your group may treat these things in a light hearted manner, one person might be connecting at a deeper level. Be prepared to offer support for anyone who wants to talk further. Discuss with your church leader any situations that may require further attention.

00.00

DOWNLOAD... *Refreshments*

00.10

NETWORK... *Release The Pressure*

Stand each member of the group in a line at one end of the room. Give each one a quality balloon (much easier to blow up). Give out some pens (biros will normally do, but check this out in advance – marker pens and ohp pens are great) and ask them to mark the balloon with their name.

Give them 30 seconds to inflate the balloon as fully as they can without it bursting. Instruct them not to tie the balloon. Then on your signal, ask them to hold the balloon out and to let the air out. Wait until all the balloons have come to earth and then work out which balloon made the best progress across the room.

If there is a tie, repeat the exercise with the remaining contestants as a final.

Play subsequent rounds as time allows.

00.15

MAIL... *Intro and Messages*

Have a balloon handy to illustrate as you introduce the theme of the session.

SAY:

- We all know how it feels to be angry. Usually it starts small and builds up.
- It can be like a balloon waiting to burst, and then when someone pushes us just that little bit more we explode. We all have a breaking point.
- But is it wrong? Have we got a right to get angry when we're being wrongly treated? Let's see what you think.

Ask the group to vote true or false on the following statements:

- Anger is the sign of an inflated ego and is always wrong *(True/False)*
- Anger comes from our sense of justice and can be appropriate *(True/False)*
- Anger can be dangerous and should be suppressed *(True/False)*
- It's O.K. to take your anger out on things that don't have feelings *(True/False)*
- Suppressed anger leads to stress and emotional problems – we should express it *(True/False)*

www.browse

00.20

START UP... Slo-mo Charades

Divide the group into two teams. The teams take it in turns to send a volunteer to the front to act out a situation in which they get angry, and the team has to guess the situation. The special rule is that all actions must be done in slow motion. Do a quick demonstration of slow motion running for the amusement of the crowd!

Award each team 10 points for a correct guess within a minute and 20 points if within the first 30 seconds.

- ö Your kid sister is scribbling on your school work.
- ö Someone is using your game console without permission.
- ö Someone spills ketchup on your best coat.
- ö A friend is making fun of your haircut.
- ö The bus goes straight past without stopping.
- ö Your team mate won't pass to you.
- ö A car drives through a puddle and you get soaked.
- ö You stub your toe on the table leg.

00.30

MEGA BITE... Slow To Anger

READ: **Psalm 103:8–10**

SAY:

- ö There are some things in the Bible that surprise us. God shows himself to have a character that sometimes differs from our expectations. For example, the Bible says that he gets jealous – that he won't share us with anyone else: but we are used to seeing jealousy as a bad thing.
- ö And here we find out that he gets angry. That suggests that anger is not always wrong. But the key thing here is that anger is not God's first reaction.

Human anger is impulsive. But God's anger is slow, and can be overcome by love. That tells us something about how our anger should be.

00.34

NETWORK... Count To Ten (SG)

Sit everyone in a circle. If you have groups of more than 15, divide into groups of 8 12. Ask everyone to close their eyes, and give them the challenge of counting to 10. The rules are simple. Anyone may speak at any time. They may only say one number at a time. And only one person may say each number. If two people speak at the same time, you must start again at 1. The aim is to count to ten as fast as possible – but with no repeating sequences being allowed.

It's often much more difficult than it sounds, but if your team manage it straight away. Challenge them to count to 20.

00.39

MEGA BITE... Quick Slow Slow

ASK: What is the secret of success in that game?

It only works because most of the group sits quietly for most of the time.

READ: **James 1:19–21**

ASK:

- ö What should we be quick to do?
- ö What should we be slow to do?

James expands this thought on anger to apply to our speech generally. Not only should we avoid blowing our top in an instant, we should be people who always listen more than we speak. We should always look to guard our tongue.

Perhaps the first step in curbing a fiery temper is to cultivate the art of listening before speaking!

00.44

CHATROOM... Wind Up Classics (SG)

PREPARATION: Draw a circle on a large sheet of paper and write the following phrases as rays coming out from the sun.

- ö Getting stuck with your schoolwork
- ö Your parents being unreasonable
- ö Being teased about who you fancy
- ö Having something precious stolen
- ö Being falsely accused
- ö Having fun poked at your accent/laugh
- ö Not having enough money
- ö Your football team losing

ACTIVITY: Ask everyone to have a good look at the situations described and to identify which of them is the most sure to wind them up. Then work round each person in the group. Ask everyone else to guess which one that person would have chosen, before they talk about it themselves.

www.shutdown

00.50

SAVE... Smoothing It Over (SG)

READ: **Ephesians 4:26**

SAY: Paul teaches that if we hold on to our anger, it becomes a foothold for the devil, something that can give him entry into our relationships, from which he can cause more damage/sin.

ACTIVITY: Give each member of your group a piece of paper with a circle in the middle and lines coming out from the centre like rays of the sun. Ask them to write on each ray the name of a different person whom they are close to.

Then invite them to work through each ray at a time and to spend a moment thinking, 'Is there anything they have done to annoy me that we never cleared up?' Encourage them not to spend too long on each one – the idea is not to dredge up loads of old mistakes, but to see if there is any anger we are harbouring today. Ask them, if there is someone whom they know has made them angry recently, to add them to the list.

00.56

ON LINE... Letting It All Out

Give each individual a deflated balloon to hold. As they hold it ask them to think through the past week and particularly about those few occasions when they have felt angry. As they think of each incident ask them to blow one puff of air into their balloon – the size of puff determined by how angry they felt. The idea is not to have the most inflated balloon but to remind us that pressure does build up.

Then to conclude, have everyone let their balloon deflate while asking God to remove the anger, apologising if our anger caused us to sin and forgiving those who hurt/frustrated us.

CLOSE...

End

rs 2

MENU

HOW TO BE A HERO

True heroism

www.logon

Download	Refreshments
Network	Hero's Welcome
Mail	Intro and Messages

www.browse

Start-Up*	Who's The Greatest?
Network	From Fan to Obsession
Mega Bite	Heroes of Faith
Network	Can U Handle It?
Mega Bite	Surrounded by Heroes
Network	Fitness Test
Mega Bite*	Eye Glue

www.shutdown

Save	Hero's Hour
On-Line	Coach to Coach
Close	

140 130 120 110 100 90 80 70 60 50 40 30 20 10

(SG) = small group activities, led by a member of the team.

**Eliminate for 45 minute programme.*

AIM TO TEACH

That we must choose our role models carefully. That faith is the key to true heroism.

AIM THAT THE GROUP SHOULD

Consider their own strengths and weaknesses. Ask for God's help in taking a practical step of heroism.

rs 2

www.logon

00.00

DOWNLOAD... *Refreshments*

00.10

NETWORK... *Hero's Welcome*

Invite the group to audition as extras for the next Hollywood block buster. Explain that you are about to test out their skills by getting them to act out their reaction when different people enter the room.

Choose five suitable celebrities that are guaranteed to provoke different reactions among the public. Arrange for some volunteers to enter the room, one at a time, dressed as famous people. If costumes are too hard to come by, you could create the same situation, simply by carrying in a large sign showing the name of the celebrity and asking the group to use their imagination.

00.16

MAIL... *Intro and Messages*

SAY:

ö Your reactions show that we form opinions about people in the public eye.

ö Some people we admire, and some we despise, without really knowing them.

ö But what is it that makes someone worthy of our respect and adulation?

Forward →

www.browse

00.18

START UP... Who's The Greatest?

Ask for five volunteers. Give them each a sign to hold bearing the names of one of the five American heroes described below. Then give them the relevant brief account of their heroism to read to the group.

SAY: Here are some stories of modern day American Heroes. Listen to their stories and decide on who you think is the greatest hero.

1. John McCain crashed in Vietnam. His arms were broken, his leg mangled. He was a prisoner for years. When he came out, he was asked, *'How did it feel when you heard Americans were protesting the war?'* He said, *'I thought that's what we were fighting for – the right to protest.'*

   A hero who understands the real enemy deserves heroic accolades.
2. Abraham Lincoln. He staged national repentance days. Another leader would not do that, or would demoralise his side if he did. And yet, somehow, Lincoln had the gift of inspiring, while demanding a quite fierce moral scrutiny.
3. Sarah and Jim Brady became quiet but consistent voices for gun control after part of Jim's brain was blasted away when John Hinckley attempted to assassinate the then President Reagan.

   Mrs. Brady has been called a liar and a Nazi by hecklers at her public appearances.
4. Frances Davis, a Brooklyn mother who has waged an all-out crusade against inner-city violence. She comes to crusading out of horror. In the six years between 1987 and 1993, three of her sons were murdered in separate incidents on the streets of Bedford-Stuyvesant.
5. Richard Jewell, the 34-year-old security guard who was for months suspected of bombing Centennial Park in Atlanta during the Summer Olympics before the FBI finally cleared him, says of his experience: *'My life disintegrated in the snap of a finger, the exhale of a breath.'* Jewell says he will go down in history known as 'the former suspect.' Jewell did what heroes do: he found a bomb, notified authorities, and helped clear the endangered area – all heroic actions. 'And one more thing. He paid for it.'

Ask the group to line up behind the person who they consider to be the greatest hero. Invite anyone to give reasons for their choice. What does this suggest it means to be a true hero?

00.25

NETWORK... From Fan to Obsession

PREPARATION: Make a selection of stars cut out from card. On each card write one of the actions on the list below.

- ö Paying £50 for a rare CD
- ö Refusing to wash because you shook hands with them
- ö Queuing all night for the best seats at a concert
- ö Stealing the rubbish from outside their house for valuable information
- ö Creating a tribute in your bedroom
- ö Changing your name to theirs
- ö Trying to convince your friends that they are the most talented person on the planet
- ö Buying 5 copies of each single to try to boost their chart rating
- ö Refusing to record over any video of their TV appearances

ACTIVITY: Divide into teams of 4 or 5. Give each team a complete set of cards and a piece of string. Ask them to lay the string down on the floor as the dividing line between acceptable actions and those that seem more like an obsession.

Each team should then proceed to spread out the stars on the floor in relation to the string.

Discuss the results.

DEBRIEF:

- ö Is being fanatical about any other person really damaging, or is it all just harmless fun?
- ö It's easy to get the idea that having heroes must be a bad idea. But it's good to have role models, to have an ambition to be like someone great.
- ö It just really depends on which heroes you choose.

00.30

MEGA BITE... Heroes of Faith

PREPARATION: Create some certificates with the wording:

The Official World Council of Heroes and Villains

Certificate of Heroism

This is to certify that ________________________________

has been found worthy to be called a TRUE HERO because

____

ACTIVITY: In the same teams ask the young people to take a closer look at some possible heroes. Give each team one of the following Bible passages and one of the certificates to fill in on that Bible 'hero'.

1. **Hebrews 11:4–7**
2. **Hebrews 11:8–12**
3. **Hebrews 11:17–22**
4. **Hebrews 11:23–31**

Ask them to look at the main character and fill in the blanks. Make clear that if they do not think that any of the characters deserve to be seen as heroic they should say so and why.

Feedback by asking each group to read out their finished certificates.

00.35

NETWORK... Can U Handle It?

SAY: Imagine that you're all together facing the following challenges. It's up to you to volunteer to handle each situation on behalf of your friends.

Read out, one at a time, a list similar to the one below. Ask the group members to stand up if they are willing to take responsibility for the group in these areas. After the first person has stood, invite any others to stand if they would be willing to step in if the other person failed. Ask anyone who thinks that they could never volunteer under any circumstances to say so.

Removing a spider from the bath

Climbing into an upstairs window when the family's locked out

Leading a school assembly

Joining the army during a war

Taking the blame for a friend in trouble

Going to the police after witnessing a burglary

You could add to this list by choosing a situation that an individual has to respond to there and then. But they didn't know about this before they actually stood up.

00.40

OMEGA BITE... Surrounded by Heroes (SG)

This could be done as a discussion or a '1 Minute Round'.

READ: **Hebrews 12:1–3**

1. Who are the 'great cloud of witnesses'?
2. Life is like a race. What advice is given on how to run it?
3. What did Jesus have to put up with?
4. What was his inspiration?
5. How should we learn from him?

00.45

NETWORK... Fitness Test

Derive an appropriate fitness test for your group. Ask for two volunteers to take part in it. If you have a group full of sport mad lads (or ladettes), a straight press up or running contest would do. For the more sedate you could have two volunteers lean against a wall and then bend their knees until their thighs are perpendicular to the wall, holding the position for the maximum time. Designate a coach to each contestant, whose job it is to keep them motivated, encouraging them to win.

Promise and supply a good prize for the winner to share with their coach.

ASK:

ö Does it help having someone spurring you on?

ö Can you think of a time when you have had to work hard to keep going?

ö What was your motivation?

00.50

OMEGA BITE... Eye Glue (SG)

READ: **Hebrews 12:1–3**

SAY: It's much easier to get motivated when we can see our reward. Jesus endured more than we can possibly imagine on the cross, and the Bible says it was because of the joy ahead of him.

ASK: If you were completely confident that one day you would be with God in his paradise, do you think you would live differently? How?

www.shutdown

00.55

SAVE... Hero's Hour (SG)

PREPARATION: Have the following list of actions viewed on a large sheet of paper or OHP.

- ö Standing up against something that is wrong
- ö Helping someone who has no-one else to help them
- ö Persevering under pressure
- ö Trusting God when there seems no way out
- ö Suffering for someone else
- ö Doing what's right when people laugh at you
- ö Giving something away without being noticed

Ask the group to sit quietly and choose one which they feel is a challenge they are needing to act on at the moment.

00.58

ON LINE... Coach to Coach

Have everyone sit in a pair and share which statement from the list they feel challenged about at the moment.

If the group can handle it have them pray for each other (aloud or in silence). Otherwise a leader could conclude the meeting with a prayer.

CLOSE...

End

THE CLONE ZONE

MENU

Peer pressure

www.logon

Download	Refreshments
Network	Runaround
Mail	Intro and Messages

www.browse

Start-Up	Odd One Out
Chatroom*	Teen Clone Zone
Mega Bite	They Think it Strange!
Chatroom	Real Life Pressure
Network	Faith in Action
Chatroom*	Route Planner

www.shutdown

Save	Water Pressure
On-Line	Peer Prayer
Close	

(SG) = small group activities, led by a member of the team.

*Eliminate for 45 minute programme.

AIM TO TEACH

That living as Christians we must expect opposition. That if we always follow the crowd, we'll end up in hell.

AIM THAT THE GROUP SHOULD

Consider some real life situations where going God's way makes them stand out. Explore how they may find support from this group.

www.logOn

00.00

DOWNLOAD... Refreshments

00.10

NETWORK... Runaround

PREPARATION: Label three of the walls of the room (A), (B) and (C).

ACTIVITY: Play a version of this ancient TV kids quiz show. Read out each question in turn and get the group members to stand by the wall that represents the correct answer. After they have made their first choice and can see where everyone else is standing, give them 5 seconds to change their mind in 'Runaround' time. Then announce the correct answer. Everyone not standing by the correct answer either sits out, or gets no points for that question depending on your preferred rule. Then the game continues. To add spice to the action you could demand that the kids have only 5 seconds to choose their first answer as well – or they're eliminated.

1. **What is the capital of Peru?**
   A. Lima B. Leon C. Mexico City
2. **How many squares are there on a chessboard?**
   A. 48 B. 56 C. 64
3. **Who was the prime minister before Tony Blair?**
   A. John Major B. William Hague C. Margaret Thatcher
4. **What is the most common element in the earths crust?**
   A. Iron B. Aluminium C. Copper
5. **Which of these weights is equivalent to a pound?**
   A. 454g B. 568g C. 687g
6. **Who first had a hit with Eternal Flame?**
   A. The Bracelets B. The Bangles C. The Jewells
7. **Which of the following is a primary colour?**
   A. Green B. Orange C. Yellow
8. **Which football team plays at St Marys?**
   A. Sunderland B. Charlton Athletic C. Southampton
9. **Which of the following was an original member of the Eastenders cast?**
   A. Adam Woodyatt B. Todd Carty C. Steve McFadden
10. **How much would you win for getting 8 questions correct on 'Who wants to be a millionaire'?**
    A. £64,000 B. £16,000 C. £8,000

MAIL... Intro and Messages

SAY:

- ö When it's hard, it's tempting just to go along with whatever everyone else thinks.
- ö It's like you cannot fail to be influenced by everyone else.
- ö But sometimes when you're sure you're right, you need the courage to stick to your guns.

READ: **Matthew 7:13, 14**

SAY: These verses imply that If all you ever do is follow the crowd in everything, you'll end up in hell.

www.browse

00.20

START UP... Odd One Out

Ask for six volunteers. Give them each a quote similar to those listed below (the more specific the better). After they have read out their quote invite the group to boo hiss and jeer in proportion to how much abuse they think they would get from their peers for making that admission.

I love... (a band everyone else thinks is pants)

I support... (a football team no-one else does)

I wear... (shoes that no-one else would be seen in)

I really enjoy... (a really strange hobby)

I speak with a... (an accent which other people find it hard to understand)

I have my hair... (an embarrassing hair style)

From the audience reaction, work out which is the most difficult of ways to stand out from the crowd.

SAY:

- ö When we're different from the crowd it can feel very uncomfortable.
- ö Whoever we are, we all come up against pressure to fit in, wherever we live, whatever we do.
- ö And some times it makes sense not to deliberately make yourself stand out.
- ö But there are some things that matter too much to follow the crowds.

00.25

CHATROOM... Teen Clone Zone (SG)

PREPARATION: Produce a picture of a likely looking teenager (one for each team), or just a person outline labelled 'The Typical Teenager'. Spread around it several empty speech bubbles.

ACTIVITY: Put the group into teams and give each team one of the outlines. Have someone in each team to write as they design together an example of the stereotypical young person.

In each of the speech bubbles they should write a young person's view on:

family, the opposite sex, ambition, school, God, their favourite words.

ASK:

- ö Can you see any of the typical young person's attitudes in yourself?
- ö Are you typical or unusual?
- ö Are there any ways in which you would like to fit in with a person like that?

00.32

MEGA BITE... They Think it Strange! (SG)

READ: 1 Peter 4:1–5

ASK:

ö What experience of Jesus should Christians expect to share?

ö What should we live our lives for?

ö How might people react if we don't join them in sin?

ö What's wrong with living that way?

00.38

CHATROOM... Real Life Pressure (SG)

Discuss each of these situations in turn and ask the group to consider how much in real life they would be prepared to resist the pressure.

1. **You're at your friend's house for a party and they've decided to raid the drinks cabinet. The host has filled a tray with glasses of vodka and everyone has taken one. He comes to you. Do you:**

   A. Say 'Cheers' and down it in one

   B. Accept it gratefully and pretend to sip it gently, hoping that no-one will notice

   C. Politely refuse and try to change the subject

   D. Give everyone a lecture on the evils of drink

2. **You're having a sleepover and everyone's on the floor in sleeping bags and staring out into the night. You're getting the giggles. They start taking it in turns to tell dirty jokes. It comes to your turn, do you:**

   A. Join in and tell the rudest joke you can think of

   B. Pretend to be asleep

   C. Tell a tame joke and hope you get away with it

   D. Announce that you are disgusted by their filth

3. **Crossing a car park at night with some mates you spot some shopping trolleys outside a supermarket. Everyone grabs one and starts having gladiator style duels using trolleys as weapons. Do you:**

   A. Join in, after all, you're not hurting anyone

   B. Feign injury and opt out

   C. Try to drag people off to do something else

   D. Walk away shouting at how irresponsible they are

00.43

NETWORK... *Faith in Action*

PREPARATION: Place five bowls of equal size around the room labelled with 'Christian Union', 'R.E.', 'Assembly', 'Geek', 'Camp' to represent the five following situations:

- ø Explaining that this lunchtime you'll be attending a group for Christians.
- ø Joining in a discussion in an R.E. lesson, defending the Christian point of view.
- ø Describing how you came to believe in Jesus as part of an assembly.
- ø Spending your lunchtime befriending the school geek.
- ø Talking about why you went on a Christian camp to Wales instead of to Ibiza.

ACTIVITY: Give everyone a plastic cup full of water. Read out and describe the above five situations the group may face at school, involving making a stand for their faith in front of their peers.

SAY: If you had to face all these five situations in a week, how much strength would they each require?

Invite them to pour some water into each bowl in proportion to how hard they think it would be to stand up to peer pressure.

00.48

CHATROOM... *Route Planner (SG)*

PREPARATION: On a large sheet of paper draw a broad road, with a narrow road leading off to the side. On sticky labels write the following words.

Popularity	Happiness	Purpose	Excitement
Truth	Eternal Life	Acceptance	Risk
Character	Success	God's Will	Freedom

ACTIVITY: Discuss with the group whether these things are more likely to be found by following the crowd or by going God's way. Stick the label on the appropriate part of the picture in each case.

SAY:

- ö When we're under pressure, we feel like unless we do what everyone else does and says, then we'll be giving up any all chance of being happy and making a success of our lives.
- ö Real life is not so straight forward. True happiness only comes from living the way we were created to live. And that's by pleasing our maker.

www.shutdown

00.53

SAVE... Water Pressure

PREPARATION: This will only work if you have a hard floor from which water is easy to mop up.

Tie five spoons onto individual strips of toilet roll. Tie a sixth one onto three strips of toilet roll that have been plaited together. Hang all six strips from a table so that the spoons are dangling about one foot off the ground.

ACTIVITY: Ask for six volunteers who fancy a go at shooting a water pistol. Give all six a water pistol (each with a similar pay load) and set them the task of shooting through their assigned strip of toilet roll so that the spoon falls to the ground with a clang. The first to achieve this task wins (a free toilet roll).

DEBRIEF:

- ö Hopefully, the strip that was plaited shows itself to be stronger than the others.
- ö Quote **Ecclesiastes 4:12** pointing out that with Jesus we can be very strong – but this verse implies that good friendship being added helps us withstand pressure even more.
- ö Therefore as young Christians we should look out for each other, encourage each other and point it out if we're going to mess up big time.

00.58

ON LINE... Peer Prayer (SG)

SAY: Standing for Jesus is not all one-way traffic. Your Christian friends can support you and encourage you to stand up for God. In that way, peer pressure can work for you, and you can pray for one another.

Invite every group member in turn to take a seat in the middle of the room, and give everyone else 30–60 seconds to pray for them. If you have group members confident to speak out their prayers, encourage them to keep it short in order to give everyone a chance to contribute to the peer experience. But even if no-one wants to pray aloud, it can be a valuable group building experience.

CLOSE...

End

2rs MENU

THE PARTY SPIRIT

Parties and alcohol

www.logon

Download	It's Party Time
Network	Party Police
Mail	Intro and Messages

www.browse

Start-Up	Party Animal Quiz
Mega Bite	Children of Light
Chatroom	Your Mother Should Know
In-Put*	The Power of Association
Network	In a Spin
Mega Bite	Staying Sober
Network*	Taste Test

www.shutdown

Save	Positive Alternatives
On-Line	Party out the Door
Close	

(SG) = small group activities, led by a member of the team.

**Eliminate for 45 minute programme.*

AIM TO TEACH

That living as Christians is about goodness, righteousness and truth. That we must be willing to associate with all people without copying all they do. That instead of getting drunk, we can be full of God's spirit and party!

AIM THAT THE GROUP SHOULD

Discuss the right attitude to alcohol. Consider some positive alternatives to the dodgy party.

www.logon

00.00

DOWNLOAD... It's Party Time

Go to town this week on refreshments. Have some food and drink available, without spending too much money, make a special effort. Blow up some balloons and have some streamers or party poppers to share out. Bring in a good sound system and have music playing. Have some table lamps with coloured bulbs to add to the atmosphere, or some disco lights if they are available.

00.10

NETWORK... Party Police

PREPARATION: WHEN the party is in full swing, arrange for some 'officers in uniform' to burst in, and order everybody to freeze. In the mean time they should stamp on the balloons, turn the music off and start clearing away the food into bin liners, turn on the normal lights and bring the party to a close. Have them announce that they've heard that people are enjoying themselves and it's very dangerous and it's got to stop right now. Then let them leave as quickly as they arrived.

SAY:

- Today we are going to look at a Christian response to parties.
- Some people think that God is like the chief of the party police - and that he's out to spoil our fun.
- But the truth is, God invented partying and he's the expert – Heaven is described as a party.
- We just need to learn (from the master) how to do it properly.

00.15

MAIL... Intro and Messages

www.browse

00.18

START UP... Party Animal Quiz

Give each member of the group a pen and some scrap paper on which to write their answers to the following quiz.

1. **Do you have a party piece (e.g. some way of amusing, entertaining or impressing people when the moment is right)?**

   A. Oh yes, loads.

   B. I can do a couple of interesting things.

   C. I don't need a party trick.

   D. What?

2. **What kind of role do you take at a party?**

   A. the entertainer.

   B. the sidekick.

   C. the scene shifter.

   D. the audience.

3. **Have you ever won at Truth or Dare?**

   A. I'm the defending champion.

   B. I've won once.

   C. I always drop out at the last stage.

   D. I avoid those games like the plague.

4. **At the end of a long night are you more likely to say.**

   A. I really fancy you gorgeous!

   B. You are my bestest friend ever!

   C. Why did the chicken cross the road?

   D. Can we go home now?

5. **Which party animal do you most resemble?**

   A. Bucking Bronco.

   B. Laughing Hyena.

   C. Cuddly Koala.

   D. Hibernating Hedgehog.

6. **When one of your favourite songs comes on do you...**

   A. Raise your arms above your head and boogie?

   B. Try to sing along?

   C. Nod your head in time with the music?

   D. Say 'I like this song'?

7. **What are we most likely to find you doing at a party?**

   A. dancing on the tables.

   B. laughing in a big group.

   C. having a deep and meaningful chat.

   D. sulking behind the sofa.

8. **What do you do when the party's dying down?**

A. Drag everyone outside for a street party

B. Head off out to the chippy with some mates

C. Reach for the trivial pursuit

D. Go home

9. **Are you a good dancer?**

A. I can get down with the best of 'em

B. I've got two good moves and stick to what I know

C. Only if it's dark

D. I don't do dancing

10. **How do you dress for a party?**

A. I never wear the same outfit twice

B. I spend time selecting the right look for an event

C. I wear what I feel natural in

D. I dress so as to blend in with the wallpaper.

After you have read out all the questions, ask the group members to give a score for each question as follows. a. 5 points b. 3 points c. 1 point d. 0 points. Then they can add up the score and receive their party animal rating below.

40–50: Life and Soul. You are the key that gets the party swinging. You know how to have a good time and you can teach others too! But when your mates are having their hearts broken, don't expect to be the first to know!

25–40: Up For It. When the party's in full flow, you're right in the mix. But when everything's a bit flat, there's not much you can do to turn it around. You'd rather go with the flow, and just take it as it comes.

12–25: Mellow Fellow. Your idea of a good time is a cosy vid and pizza with your mates, rather than shaking your thing in the public eye. You are quite a cool customer, you just prefer to avoid the limelight.

11 or less: Damp Squib. As far as you're concerned three's a crowd and most of the time you're too busy washing your hair to step into the social whirl. It only takes a double episode of your favourite soap to make you stop in for the night.

N.B. Please treat this quiz and their verdicts with the contempt they deserve!

00.26

MEGA BITE... Children of Light

READ: **Ephesians 5:8–14**

SAY: Whether we like parties or not, our attitude to them and to what goes on at them should be shaped by our attitude to life as Christians. The key expression in this passage is... live as 'Children of Light', which, as Paul explains, means living in goodness, righteousness and truth. So, how exactly do the children of light get down on a Friday night?

00.29

CHATROOM... *Your Mother Should Know*

Ask everyone to stand up. Get them to picture the scene. You're about to set out for a party at a friend's house. You are talking to the person who looks after you at home, explaining to them honestly what you expect the party to be like. If you volunteer the following information, do you think you'll be allowed to go?

Read out the following one at a time. If they think they'll be allowed to go they should move to the right. If not, they should move to the left.

It's a pyjama party.

It's his 18th birthday party.

We've been asked to bring 8 cans of beer each.

His parents are away and don't know we're using the house.

His best mate says there will be e's and speed available.

The music will be mainly old skool hip hop with explicit lyrics.

It's a video party. We're watching an 18 movie.

It finishes at 1am.

When you have gone through the list ask them to think again. Repeat the exercise, this time asking in each case, whether they think they should be allowed to go to a party, given the details.

SAY: There may be some situations that are safe and legal but should still be avoided. As we shall see, this is not the same as being a square, or a party pooper. It's just common sense.

00.34

IN PUT... *The Power of Association*

SAY: Some party guests have only come to cause trouble. You really don't want them turning up, but you may not know what they're up to until it's too late. So should you not go to a party just in case some trouble makers turn up?

READ: **Ephesians 5:11**

Paul says have nothing to do with the deeds of darkness. So perhaps we shouldn't be at parties where dodgy stuff goes on, just in case we get associated with it or worse, get dragged into it.

READ: **1 Corinthians 5:9–11**

Who we associate with has a powerful effect on us. Parents often accuse people of having a 'bad influence' on their children. And it can be true. But our task as Christians is not to avoid all contact with people who do wrong. To do that we'd have to move to Mars! So the basic principle has to be this: be with people where they are (on the whole), but don't do everything they do.

00.37

NETWORK... *In a Spin*

PREPARATION: Divide into teams of 5 or 6. Have each team line up on one wall, facing the opposite wall of the room. Give each team a hockey stick and a large plastic ball.

ACTIVITY: On your signal, the first player dribbles the ball with the hockey stick across the room. When he reaches the other side he touches the curve of the hockey stick on the ground, such that the handle is vertical, places his forehead on the top of the stick, and then walks around the hockey stick ten times. The stick should remain in an upright position for all ten turns. (Be careful with this one, participants do get very dizzy-children prone to dizzy spells should sit this one out!)

Then they must simply return the ball and the stick to the next player in their team. It's not as easy as it sounds.

00.43

MEGA BITE... *Staying Sober*

READ: **Ephesians 5:15–18**

SAY: Hitting a ball across the room with a stick sounds easy. But when your head's in a spin, it's hard to stay on your feet, let alone hit a moving target!

That's a bit like alcohol. Even when people have one drink, their reaction times for things like driving are affected. Some people have been convicted for drink driving, when tested after only half a glass of wine. It just shows that, while some people think that they can take their alcohol, even small amounts do affect our thinking.

Apostle Paul says that we are to be wise and to make the most of every opportunity. Sometimes we can't make the most of it if we've been drinking. We couldn't take someone to hospital in an emergency if we've been drinking. We may not be best able to give advice to someone who is upset, or in a good frame of mind to share our faith, if we're the worse for wear. There is more to the right attitude to alcohol than 'Don't get drunk'.

00.47

NETWORK... *Taste Test*

PREPARATION: Prepare three tumblers each containing a different type of non alcoholic beer or lager.

ACTIVITY: Explain that there are now some very good non alcoholic drinks on the market, so even if they like the taste of beer and wine, they can have it without needing alcohol. The question is, can they tell the difference. Point out that they are not supposed to gulp it down and get bladdered. Small amounts please!

Have four volunteers each taste the three samples and to try to guess which of them does NOT contain alcohol.

When they have all given their answer to which of the drinks are non-alcoholic, reveal the answer. They are all alcohol free!

(If they suss you out too early, ask them which one they prefer!)

SAY: There might be some great beers around, but staying sober doesn't have to mean missing out.

READ: **Ephesians 5:18**

This verse does not read 'Don't get drunk, don't have a good time, and always carry a clean handkerchief!.' Some people think that the Bible just gives us a list of don'ts. The truth is, for every 'don't' there is a positive alternative. Something good to do instead.

READ: **Ephesians 5:18** says don't get drunk on wine, instead [get drunk on] the spirit. That's literally what it means. Let God's life in you be your reason to party, your power to celebrate, and your freedom to be happy.

www.shutdown

00.53

SAVE... Positive Alternatives

Challenge the group to prove positive points throughout their teenage years. Instead of just doing what everyone else does, they should invite their friends to a new kind of party.

See what alternative suggestions there are to parties simply consisting of drink, music and pairing off.

Some suggestions:

- ö Camp out in your back garden
- ö Arrange a trip to the beach for a late night game of luminous frisbee.
- ö Paddling and a barbecue.
- ö Hire out a bouncy castle or inflatable sumo wrestling or pole jousting.
- ö Organise a murder mystery party with fancy dress.

00.56

ON LINE... Party out the Door

Get hold of some funky new Christian music, and pump up the sound system! Invite in the person you know with the best sense of rhythm and have them teach the whole group a new dance routine (but make it accommodating for all). End the meeting in prayer and in celebration mood, pretty much as it began.

CLOSE...

End

rs 2

MENU

ALIENATION

How to give away your faith

www.logon

Download	*Refreshments*
Network	*Chocolate Teapot*
Mail	*Intro and Messages*

www.browse

Start-Up	*Saintly Simile*
Mega Bite	*Alien Visitation*
Chatroom*	*Secret Talents*
Network	*Peter's Mallet*
Mega Bite	*On Your Marks...*
Chatroom*	*Thinking On Your Feet*

www.shutdown

Save	*Question Time*
On-Line	*Mission Link*
Close	

(SG) = small group activities, led by a member of the team.

****Eliminate for 45 minute programme.***

AIM TO TEACH

That Christians are to live among non-Christians, but abstain from certain things. That Christians need to know how to explain their faith with respect.

AIM THAT THE GROUP SHOULD

Practice defending their faith. Have the opportunity to ask questions about the Christian faith.

www.logon

00.00

DOWNLOAD... Refreshments

00.05

NETWORK... Chocolate Teapot

PREPARATION: Make a graffiti wall by covering a board with blank paper.

ACTIVITY: As the young people arrive and tuck into the refreshments, invite them to 'draw something totally useless'. Start them off with the idea – 'a chocolate teapot', and see what else they come up with (with nothing rude or offensive allowed).

00.15

MAIL... Intro and Messages

Kick off the meeting by saying that we will be returning to some useless items later!

Forward →

www.browse

00.17

START UP... *Saintly Similes*

PREPARATION: Divide the young people into two teams and stand or sit them by opposite walls of the room. Place two chairs in the middle of the room labelled 'True' and 'False' respectively.

Number off the members of each team, such that each one has a player 1, a player 2, a player 3 etc.

ACTIVITY: Read out one of the words from the list below then call out a number. Ask the group to decide instantly whether they think the Bible uses that word to describe a Christian. The player with the number called should give the team answer by sitting on the appropriate chair. The player to the correct chair wins a point for their team. Be ready to subtract points for violent conduct!

LIST: TRUE: Soldiers, Farmers, Branches, Sheep, Athletes, Instruments, Light, Priests, Children, Slaves, Stones, Aliens

LIST: FALSE: Tables, Pens, Shoes, Doors, Roads, Flowers, Doves, Cows.

00.23

MEGA BITE... *Alien Visitation*

Put on some spooky space-age music, dim the lights, have someone dress up as an alien (a mask and some green face paint can work wonders) and walk through the meeting room, unannounced beckoning the group to follow him!

SAY: This morning we are inviting you to take on the lifestyle of an alien!

READ: **1 Peter 2:11, 12**. Read the passage aloud twice.

SAY: Living as an alien means 'abstaining'. That is, deciding to stay out of sinful desires, which seem to be a part of life for a native!

The picture of an alien or a stranger, simply presents the fact that Christians do not belong in this world, they are just visitors. From all the images we have already looked at, the Bible repeatedly states that there are many things that set the Christian apart from the non-Christian. Even if they look and dress the same, as far as God is concerned they are totally different.

00.26

CHATROOM... *Secret Talents (SG)*

Divide the group into pairs. Ask them to share with their partner something that they can do or are good at, that not everyone in the group would know. (E.g. washing up, changing a nappy, playing the spoons, an impression, a contortion trick).

Then get each pair to join up with another pair to form a team and to decide on who has the most incredible hidden talent in their team.

One at a time, the groups should stand at the front, read out their hidden talent, and ask the rest of the audience to identify the one to whom that talent belongs. The team whose talent is correctly guessed by the fewest people wins!

CHOCOLATE TEAPOT DEBRIEF

Draw out some of the more surprising talents. Point out how amazing it is that there should be so much that has been kept hidden.

Point the group members to the graffiti wall full of useless objects.

SAY: There are lots of good ideas there, but you missed out the most useless thing of all. When we have something good that we can do and share with others, we should let people see it. The best thing that anyone can have is a relationship with God. That means the most useless thing of all is a secret Christian!

READ: **1 Peter 2:12**, drawing attention to Peter's point that we need to live as public Christians.

00.32

NETWORK... Peter's Mallet (SG)

PREPARATION: Sit the group in a circle. Bring in a cushion or padded weapon for this word association game.

ACTIVITY: The game begins by the leader calling out any simple word like 'tree', for example. Then the next person in the circle has to call out an associated word, such as 'leaf'. The next person might then say 'tea', the next 'coffee', the next 'bean' etc. Play passes round the circle as each person must then find a word associated with the previous one.

When a player pauses or hesitates, repeats or says an unassociated word, they get a bash on the head with your chosen implement and 'lose a life'.

SAY: It's a game that makes you think quickly. Sometimes it's like that when we're put on the spot about our faith. So what does the Apostle Peter recommend?

00.40

MEGA BITE... On Your Marks... (SG)

The following could be done as small group discussion or as a whole group '1 Minute Round.'

The '1 Minute Round' is where the group have 60 seconds to answer all seven questions from what Peter says, as recorded in the passage. If they succeed they receive a bag of sweets between them. Since there's a lot of questions and a long passage, read out the questions (for familiarity purposes), then the passage before announcing the start of the 1 minute and the first question...

READ: **1 Peter 3:9–15**

1. **How should Christians respond when they are insulted?**
   With blessing
2. **What does God promise those who talk his way?**
   Blessing
3. **How does God decide who to listen to?**
   By their actions
4. **What is the most likely outcome of doing good?**
   People won't want to do you harm

5. **When should Christians be afraid?**
   Never!
6. **When should we answer questions about out faith?**
   Be ready any time!
7. **How should we answer them?**
   With gentleness and respect

00.44

☺ CHATROOM... *Thinking On Your Feet (SG)*

Divide the group in half. Ask each small group to think of:

A. One typical way of insulting a Christian.

B. One or two tricky questions about their faith.

After two minutes, introduce a role-play. Get one group to act as Christians and the other group to play the 'non-Christians', asking their questions and making their insults (but not in a way that the exercise cannot be done). Encourage the Christians to think about answering the questions with gentleness and respect and showering blessing on their accusers, whilst trying to be themselves!

Discuss the role-plays afterwards

www.shutdown

00.47

SAVE... Question Time (SG)

SAY: After the exercise above, you may have questions which you find hard to answer in a way that defends your faith. Challenge every member of your group to come up with a question about Christianity that they would like answered.

QUESTION TIME

PREPARATION: Compile a panel of 'experts' to face an intense 10 minute session of questions from your groups.

Use people skilled in this area and limit the answers to each question to 60 seconds.

For effect, sit the panel behind a desk at the front of the room. Provide them with pens and paper, a jug of water and, glasses. Position a chairperson in the centre of the panel to direct the discussion.

ACTIVITY: In order to be prepared to give an answer to people's questions, we need to know what we believe. The better we understand our faith, the more confident we can be to talk to other people about it. Part of doing what Peter says must involve finding out the answers to questions. So now we want you to ask the questions that have always bugged you but you've always been afraid to ask.

00.59

ON LINE... Mission Link

Before a leader closes in prayer, take this opportunity to publicise your next special event, encouraging all those who have been challenged by today's session to pray for and invite someone who doesn't yet know Jesus.

CLOSE...

End